Star and

The Biography of Venerable Master Hsing Yun

Adapted and Illustrated by Zheng Wen
Translated from the Chinese by Madelon Wheeler-Gibb

©2003 Buddha's Light Publishing
First edition 2003.

Published by Buddha's Light Publishing
3456 S. Glenmark Drive
Hacienda Heights, CA 91745
USA.
Tel: 626-923-5143
Fax: 626-923-5145
Email: itc@blia.org

ISBN 0-9715612-4-9
Library of Congress Control Number:2003103866

Printed in Taiwan.

table of contents

A Relaxed and Easy Way to Learn Dharma

I like to read biographies, especially those of ancient sages and wise, virtuous individuals. From their life events, thoughts, and actions, I can see the bigger picture of the historical environment in which they lived. It is also interesting to see what kind of individuals human beings have looked to for their spiritual examples. Biography serves not only to record the events of one person's life, but also to edify society at large and to benefit future generations.

When a person has spent a lifetime following a religious vocation, giving up personal affections and any desire to be rich or famous, there is a warmth and integrity that emanates from his or her upright behavior that has the capacity to evoke the truth, goodness, and beauty in human nature. Throughout the history of Buddhism in India, China, Korea, and Japan, there have been countless Buddhist monastics who have embraced great vows of compassion and have left behind an eternal, magnificent light for all human beings.

Fo Guang Cultural Enterprise Co. Ltd. has already published the *Anthology of Eminent Chinese Buddhist Monastics*. Their newest project has been the rendering of the lives of eminent monastics in a modern comic strip format of one hundred volumes. Everyone knows that pictures are more direct than words in conveying a message and making a lasting impression. Comic strips are an especially effective means of communication for teenagers since they are already familiar with them and enjoy them. Actually, I think wholesome and interesting comic strips are appealing to all ages, not just teenagers. Comic strips that are beautifully written and illustrated can be enjoyed again and again. This comic strip anthology of eminent masters can, on the one hand, join the popular trend of comics as literature while, on the other hand, it can actually guide people in their spiritual lives. Therefore, this entire anthology is worth collecting and appreciating.

The following features can be found in this set of books:

1. Warm and touching stories of eminent monastics:
The personalities, speech, and actions of these spiritual leaders no longer seem strange and remote. These stories tell the life journeys of these great masters without any preaching or rigidity. The words flow elegantly and are easy to understand, helping the readers to experience the true spirit of these individuals.

2. Lively, humorous illustrations:
These books bring together famous illustrators of all ages from Taiwan and Southeast Asia. Each strip has been rendered in the artist's own style. This format allows their wonderful gifts and talents to blossom and to be enjoyed by countless people.

3. Providing abundant and accurate information:
All the artistic details such as architecture, clothing, and Buddhist statues are rendered in an accurate, authentic fashion, which helps the reader gather historical information while reading in a relaxed manner.

4. Complete and thorough structural arrangement:
In addition to wonderful illustrations, each book contains mini-biographies, lineage history, and words of wisdom from each of the eminent monastics, helping the reader to have a better understanding of each monastic's life as well as Buddhist history and teaching.

The *Buddhist Legends of Adventure and Courage* covers a hundred monastics representing the various lineages and spans from early Indian Buddhism to contemporary Buddhist masters, all of whom have greatly contributed to the dissemination and teaching of

Buddhism. Presenting their conduct and integrity in such a lively, energetic, and fresh manner really has a positive and meaningful impact on the dissemination of Humanistic Buddhism. As a sutra says: "Offer sentient beings what they desire first so that you will be able to share the Buddha's wisdom with them."

I hope that we can make Buddhism available to more people by using this relaxed and easy format. Particularly, I hope that the presentation of role models such as eminent monastics can touch the hearts of young, impressionable teenagers and allow everyone to enjoy a beautiful, wholesome life.

Venerable Master Hsing Yun

A Master Different from Public Perception

I am very happy to have this opportunity to render Master Hsing Yun, a Humanistic Practitioner, in a comic strip biography. I specialize in rendering historical figures, so I seldom get a chance to work on contemporary topics. Therefore, when considering how to do this book, I really gave it a lot of thought, particularly when I realized that I would be drawing someone as important to Buddhism as Master Hsing Yun. I felt the responsibility and challenge was truly great. This is also the first time in my illustration career where I have actually spent more time on digesting the material and preparing the script than on the actual drawing of the scenes. As I collected the Master's books and the biography about Venerable Master Hsing Yun, I found him to be a very approachable, interesting, and tolerant individual, quite different from his portrayal in newspapers, magazines, and on television surrounded by devotees and flashing cameras.

I hope that this book provides you with a different perspective on Venerable Master Hsing Yun.

Zheng Wen
Shing Dian, Taiwan
2000

Part I
MANY HAPPY RETURNS
Lifetimes Spent with
Buddhas

Departing from the Mansion of the Golden Crane
my old friend heads west,
    Amidst the mists and blossoms of the third moon,
    sailing down to Yangzhou.
        Into the azure distance recedes
        the image of that lonely sail.
            Behind, the sight of the Yangtze flowing
            toward the sky above.

Yangzhou, city of dancing weeping willows, has been famous since ancient times. Literati from many dynasties have been attracted to its beauty. Writing and reciting poetry, and enjoying tea, they often linger in the city's lovely atmosphere, with no thought of returning home.

Yangzhou has a county nearby called...*Jiangdu.*

The spirit and vitality of this little-known place has contributed to the nurturing and cultivation of the outstanding spiritual leader, Hsing Yun.

COME ON EVERYONE, EAT UP! IT TASTES BEST WHEN IT'S SHARED!

OH MY WORD!

WHAT A FOOLISH BOY!

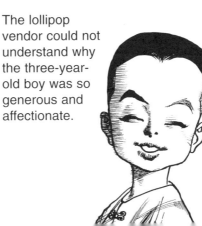

The lollipop vendor could not understand why the three-year-old boy was so generous and affectionate.

Li Guoshen

He didn't know that this young boy would become the world famous Venerable Master Hsing Yun. This boy's name was Li Guoshen, which meant "Profound Benefit to all Countries."

One night, at a family fireside gathering, an old man of the village began to tell a story...

ONCE UPON A TIME, THERE WAS A BEARDED MAN WHO LIVED ON THE MOUNTAIN...

...THE POOR MAN WAS VERY LONELY AND HUNGRY.

ONE WINDY, SNOWY NIGHT THE OLD MAN BECAME VERY SICK.

All of a sudden, Profound Benefit's sister, Simple Flower, noticed that the little boy, Profound Benefit, was missing!

?

WHERE DID MY BABY BROTHER GO?

WHERE ARE YOU? THE STORY IS NOT FINISHED YET!

PROFOUND BENEFIT

WA! WA! WA!

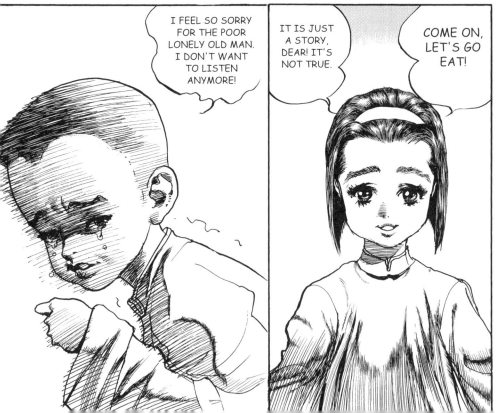

I DON'T WANT TO EAT. I WANT TO TAKE MY FOOD TO THAT POOR OLD WHITE BEARDED MAN!

BOO HOO HOO!

No matter how hard they tried, they could not persuade Profound Benefit to stop crying over the old man in the story. Suddenly his mother had an idea...

HOW ABOUT IF WE TAKE YOU TO SEE THE OLD MAN HIMSELF?

So his mother and Simple Flower took him to visit his elderly grandfather. The little toddler believed his grandfather to be the old man in the story and offered him his dinner.

WA!
WA!

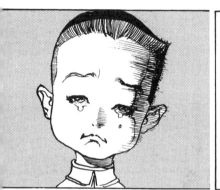

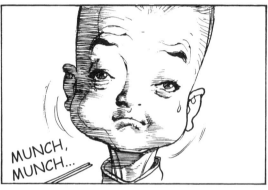

MUNCH,
MUNCH...

Now Profound Benefit was once again, a happy little boy, ready to eat!

Glad to see that the old man had enjoyed the company and his meal, Profound Benefit was at last willing to return home.

Another time, five-year-old Profound Benefit spotted a bunch of little chicks huddling together in the rain...

TAT· · · ·

TAT· · ·

...He carried them back home and placed them before the wood-burning furnace to help them dry off.

CHEEP

One little chick made a dash into the fire in panic.

CHEEP, CHEEP!

CHEEP

OH NO!
HOW AWFUL!

CHEEP,
CHEEP!

When Profound Benefit snatched it back, he found its lower beak had been burnt quite badly.

CHEEP! CHEEP!

From then on, Profound Benefit tenderly nursed the little chick...

...That little chick later grew into a healthy and happy hen, that laid several eggs a day.

As a young boy, Profound Benefit often accompanied his grandmother, who was a very devoted Buddhist, to the local temple to offer incense and pay respects to the Buddha.

After Grandmother had offered fruits, candies, and cookies at the temple...

...she would return home with a portion of the offerings, allowing the children to enjoy them along the way. This was the beginning of Profound Benefit's deep connection to Buddha.

Some time later, China found itself in the midst of war, and the everyday lives of its village people were turned upside down. One day, as a Buddhist monk walked by, Profound Benefit was greatly impressed with the calm and peaceful presence of the dignified monk in his graceful robes.

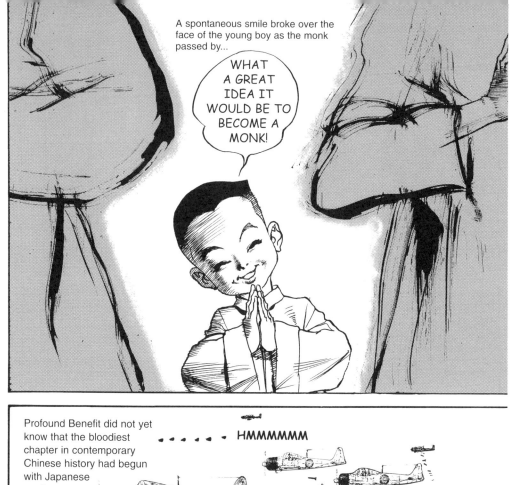

A spontaneous smile broke over the face of the young boy as the monk passed by...

WHAT A GREAT IDEA IT WOULD BE TO BECOME A MONK!

Profound Benefit did not yet know that the bloodiest chapter in contemporary Chinese history had begun with Japanese gunfire...

HMMMMMM

...at Rushing Waterways Bridge in Hebei on July 7, 1937.

BAM

POW

In those days, the people in Profound Benefit's village had to cross a canal to purchase their daily supplies. With no boats available, people would often carry others on their backs across the canal for a few pennies.

But when war broke out, no one wanted to risk their lives carrying others across just for a few cents. The rushing current of the canal was very dangerous and few dared to swim across.

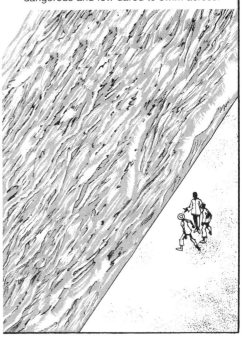

At this time, Profound Benefit was only ten years old.

WOOSH!

Yet his courage was already great. Stripping off his shirt and tying it around his forehead...

SHA!

He plunged right in!

WHOOSH

Each time he crossed, he would swim the canal in both directions, bringing home supplies for both his family and neighbors.

WHISH

THE SECOND YOUNGEST SON IN THE LI FAMILY IS QUITE A REMARKABLE KID! MAYBE HE IS GOING TO BECOME THE GREATEST IN THAT FAMILY.

PLOP!
PLOP!
PLOP!

PLOP!

In the meantime, Japanese soldiers continued their invasion of China, creating havoc and destruction everywhere they went.

...The result was that over one hundred million people found their homes in ruins and their family members missing or dead.

AHHH!

It was during these very dangerous times that Profound Benefit's father had to leave home on business. For over two years, the family received no news as to his whereabouts.

Without his father at home, young Profound Benefit and his family suffered financially.

Still, his mother never gave up hope, and when Profound Benefit was twelve years old, they set out to find his father.

The young Profound Benefit and his mother became very discouraged and sad...

...Halfway to Nanjing, Profound Benefit and his mother passed by a newly-formed regiment of Chinese soldiers practicing their drills.

23

Profound Benefit was very curious and wanted to take a look!

GREET!

In the same crowd, there was also a monk from the temple on Cloud Dwelling Mountain.

The monk noticed Profound Benefit's fresh face, ready smile, and curiosity as the boy watched the troops.

...COOL!

WOULD YOU LIKE TO BECOME ONE OF US?

SURE! O.K.!

MOTHER, I HAVE ALREADY PROMISED TO BECOME A MONK, I CANNOT GO BACK ON MY WORD.

THUD!

MOTHER, PLEASE ACCEPT MY DECISION!

CLUNK!

Allowing her young son to fulfill his wish was a real struggle for his mother. Tearfully, she finally nodded in agreement.

GOOD-BYE, MOTHER!

CLOUD DWELLING MOUNTAIN TEMPLE
His New Home

At that time, Cloud Dwelling Mountain Temple, which was over 1,500 years old, was famous far and wide.

Profound Benefit came before the monk, Vast Vows, who accepted him as his disciple.

Profound Benefit was then given his Dharma name, "Thorough Enlightenment," and his new monastic name, "Instantanous Awakening." Later, he chose the Dharma name, Hsing Yun, "Star and Cloud," for himself, with his teacher's approval.

Later, Hsing Yun would become the 48th patriarch of the Linji Chan school of Buddhism.

29

During those days of war, no one had any extra money, food, or clothing. At Cloud Dwelling Mountain Temple, Hsing Yun was penniless.

One time, Hsing Yun became very ill with malaria. First he was hot, then he was cold... all in all he suffered a lot.

But the rules in the forest monastery did not allow for any sick leave, so Hsing Yun still had to attend both morning and evening chanting.

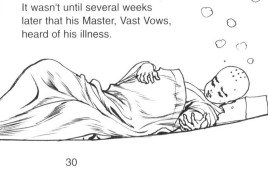

It wasn't until several weeks later that his Master, Vast Vows, heard of his illness.

IF I CAN MAKE IT POSSIBLE, NO ONE SHALL EVER GO HUNGRY!

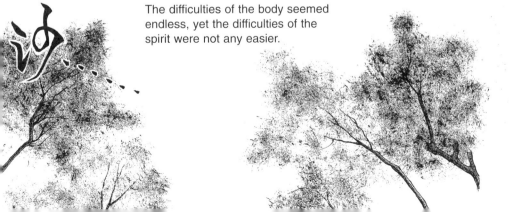

The difficulties of the body seemed endless, yet the difficulties of the spirit were not any easier.

Hsing Yun was only twelve years old when he arrived at Cloud Dwelling Mountain Temple, yet, he was required to endure three- to four-hour lectures while kneeling on gravel with joined palms.

When finally allowed to stand, he often found small stones lodged in his knees...

...and the hours endured with his palms joined left his hands rigid and stiff.

At fifteen, the teenaged Hsing Yun received full ordination, and soon learned that sometimes you can't win no matter how hard you try.

SMACK

SO, WHAT IF YOU HADN'T BEEN SENT? WOULD YOU STILL HAVE COME?

The smack of the willow twigs chased pride and stubborness from his mind, and Hsing Yun's character and commitment began to take shape.

As his personality began to form, Hsing Yun learned to be content in every situation...

...living in harmony with circumstances--carefree, yet also concerned for others.

Hsing Yun would raise his head, wondering where the sounds of mountain streams were coming from.

The next fifty-three days of post-ordination monastic training proved to be very difficult for this curious and inquisitive, young boy.

The leading master in the Precept Hall would catch him, and...

Whack! The bamboo cane would come down again across his shoulders.

SMACK

WHAT ARE YOU LISTENING TO? CLOSE YOUR EARS NOW!

YOUNG AS YOU ARE, WHAT SOUND CAN YOU POSSIBLY CLAIM TO BE YOURS?

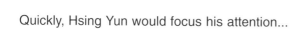

Quickly, Hsing Yun would focus his attention...

...and try not to listen to the leaves that rustled like waves and rain that beat on the eaves...

...allowing nothing to enter his ears!

OPEN YOUR EARS! WHAT SOUND CAN YOU SAY IS NOT YOURS!

Although very tough, this kind of training taught Hsing Yun to accept any and all circumstances. This actually began to help him in his practice and teaching.

Hsing Yun gradually developed the ability to be peaceful and happy with many resources or with none, whether full or hungry, whether early or late, with much or little, with winning or with losing, with big or small.

Hsing Yun lived in Cloud Dwelling Mountain Temple for six years, developing a deep and profound faith, making a vow to dedicate his entire life to Buddhism.

Part II
THE YOUNG MONK
FACES TURBULENT TIMES

Hsing Yun was accepted at Flaming Mountain Buddhist College, in Zhenjiang, in 1945. By that time, he had grown into an outstanding young monk.

Flaming Mountain Buddhist College had a very good reputation, and was considered equal to Beijing University, with outstanding teachers and students.

The Venerable Profound Completeness taught Hsing Yun the commentary on the Abhidharma.

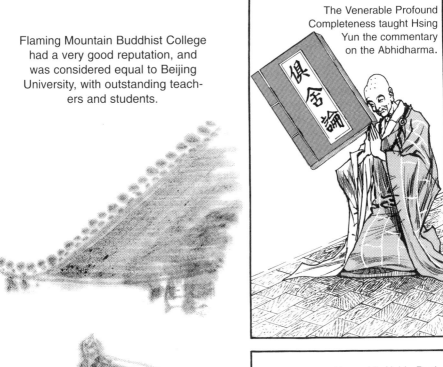

俱舍論

Venerable Noble Peak taught Hsing Yun early Buddhism.

原始佛教

Due to the Sino-Japanese war, a nearby teachers' college had been abandoned.

Left behind was a large library with hundreds of books.

The older monastics did not take any interest in it, but Hsing Yun spent hours there, preferring to read rather than to return home.

He spent hours pouring over classical Chinese literature...

...and translations of Western novels and biographies, such as **The Little Prince** and **Joan of Arc**.

Hsing Yun received his first introduction to Western thought through literature. This opened a window in his heart and mind beyond the monastery and beyond China.

Although Hsing Yun had never received a formal education, he found his days filled with the joy of study.

Ever since then, Hsing Yun has continued the practice of self-study.

Hsing Yun left Flaming Mountain Buddhist College in 1947.

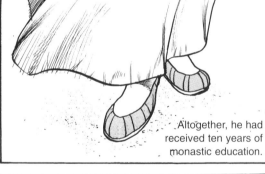

Altogether, he had received ten years of monastic education.

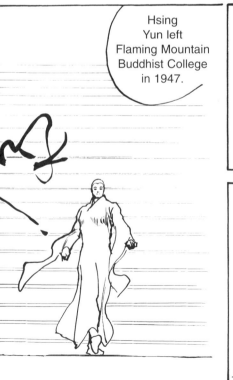

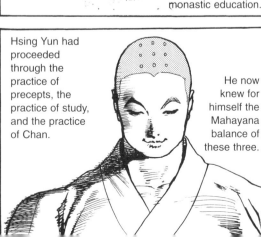

Hsing Yun had proceeded through the practice of precepts, the practice of study, and the practice of Chan.

He now knew for himself the Mahayana balance of these three.

Equipped with a youthful and enthusiastic heart, Hsing Yun confidently stepped right into the middle of an unsteady and desperate society.

He would soon find himself totally engaged in the survival of his nation and his religion.

Both Hsing Yun and his close friend, Venerable Courageous Wisdom...

...were anxious about the future of China.

WHAT ARE WE GOING TO DO? THE BEAUTIFUL RIVERS AND MOUNTAINS OF OUR COUNTRY WILL BE LOST!

HMMM... I DON'T HAVE ANY IDEA WHAT BUDDHISM'S FUTURE WILL BE.

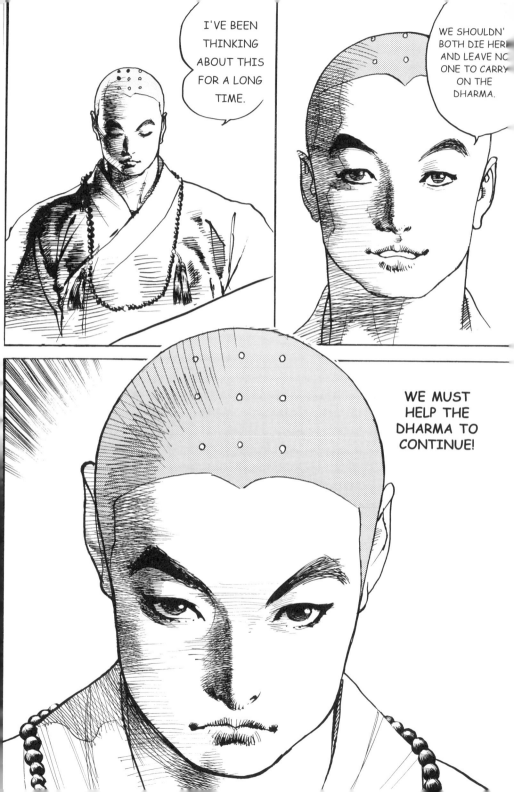

And so, Courageous Wisdom remained behind in China to defend Buddhism.

...as Hsing Yun took on the responsibility of leading a group of monastics to Taiwan.

SPLASH

SHOOSH !

The voyage would begin not only a new chapter in Hsing Yun's life, but a new chapter in the history of Chinese Buddhism.

TAT...

Arriving in Taiwan, they were immediately faced with the ravages of war.

The group quickly disbanded, each going their own way.

Hsing Yun's small bundle of personal possessions was lost during the journey, and his one extra robe he offered to his fellow monastic, Misting Cloud.

When Hsing Yun realized that everyone was astonished to see a monk with shoes...

...he took his off and walked barefoot like everyone else.

Alone, with only his thoughts as companions, Hsing Yun walked for two days from Taichung to Taipei.

When he sought shelter in different temples, he was met with "Our temple is full, we cannot take anyone in!"

...or "We cannot accept anyone from outside our province."

HEY! WE'VE WORKED REALLY HARD TO GET ENOUGH PEOPLE TO SUPPORT OUR TEMPLE...

...WHAT RIGHT DO YOU HAVE TO COME INTO OUR TERRITORY?

GET OUT OF HERE! GET LOST!

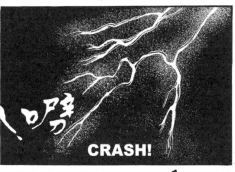

CRASH!

TAT!
TAT!
TAT!

TAT!
TAT!
TAT!

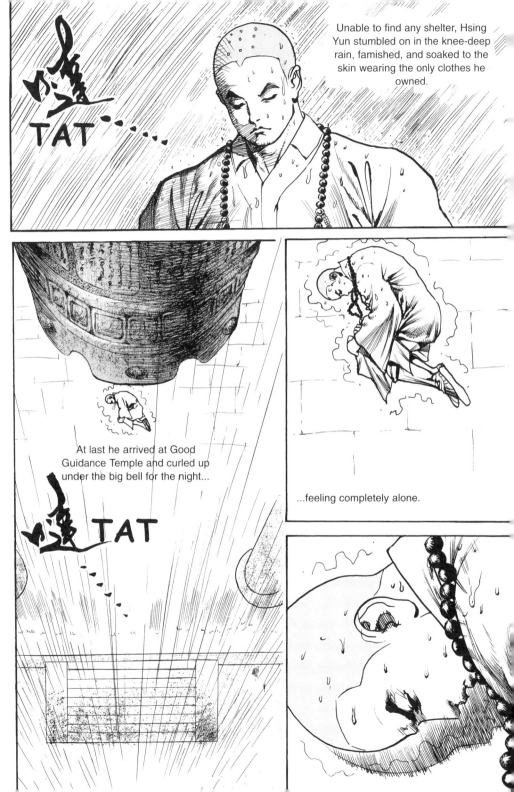

Unable to find any shelter, Hsing Yun stumbled on in the knee-deep rain, famished, and soaked to the skin wearing the only clothes he owned.

At last he arrived at Good Guidance Temple and curled up under the big bell for the night...

...feeling completely alone.

After many more difficult encounters, Hsing Yun finally arrived at Perfect Light Temple in Chungli.

Here he was met compassionately by Venerable Wondrous Fruition.

Hsing Yun worked very hard in order to repay the great kindness of Wondrous Fruition.

TAT!
TAT!
TAT!

He worked very diligently.

ZOOM!

Daily, he drew 600 pails of water from the well for the 80 or so people who lived in the monastery.

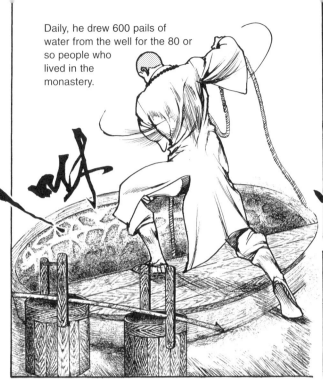

PAT! PAT! PAT!

HURRY UP! HURRY UP!

HEY! YOU MIGHT BE A BIG GUY, BUT YOU SURE AREN'T VERY FAST!

PAT

GET A MOVE ON! I KNOW LAZY GUYS WHEN I SEE THEM!

Even before daybreak, Hsing Yun had already begun his trek to the market...

...pushing the temple handcart ten miles roundtrip in order to bring back needed supplies.

NAMO AVALOKITESVARA BODHISATTVA

In the monastery, there weren't very many who were as young and strong as Hsing Yun.

He did each of his chores with energy and attention, including cleaning the bathrooms and preparing bodies for burial.

CREAK!!

One time he earned a small amount of money for helping out in a chanting service.

Immediately he bought more paper and pens to further his writing.

Even with such a heavy load of chores, Hsing Yun never gave up on his reading and writing.

He never forgot for the rest of his life, the happiness and contentment of that time.

Whenever he had free time, he would spend it, writing articles about Buddhism.

MASTER, YOU MUST GO AND WORK, OR ELSE YOU'LL STARVE.

To this day, Hsing Yun still remembers the concern of an elderly lady...

Soon they ordered several officers to watch him 24 hours a day.

However, the local police were receiving anonymous reports charging that Hsing Yun was receiving radio broadcasts from Mainland China in the day and giving out pro-communist literature at night.

DOCK!
DOCK!
DOCK!

Those who had been following him were so impressed by both his teaching and his actions, they became his devotees instead.

During his two years there, Hsing Yun developed many new associations and friendships at Perfect Light Temple.

His earnestness and diligence won him many friends and admirers.

He was highly regarded by Master Wondrous Fruition.

Master Wondrous Fruition had been an excellent teacher, and now Hsing Yun was ready to accept a larger responsibility in public life.

By observing the goings-on around him, Hsing Yun developed compassion and understanding for the people and place...

Making a plan for the future in his mind.

Part III
THE LIGHT OF HIS HEART
SHINING BRIGHTLY IN THE UNIVERSE

The next chapter of Hsing Yun's's
life began in 1952; in Ilan...

...when the local Buddhists
asked him to come and
teach.

Traveling to Ilan, in those
days, was difficult. Ilan was a
poor and remote city. After
one visit, most Dharma
teachers would never return.

Understanding Ilan's unique situation, Hsing Yun decided to stay...

...offering his services as a Dharma teacher.

CHOO, CHOOOO!

Touring the temple for the first time, Hsing Yun could see why no other Dharma teacher had been willing to stay.

...they had been turned into pillows for sleeping.

Inside, Hsing Yun found three families using the temple as their home; the cushions for kneeling were missing...

Clothing and shoes were scattered everywhere!

Soon Hsing Yun was visiting on a regular basis, offering Dharma talks that met with a lot of enthusiasm.

NO ONE REALLY CARES TO COME HERE AND TEACH.

ILAN IS SUCH A VERY POOR COUNTY

I CAN'T BELIEVE YOU ARE WILLING TO VISIT US SO REGULARLY

I NOW APOLOGIZE FOR MY COLD MANNER TOWARDS YOU WHEN YOU FIRST ARRIVED.

I WANT TO THANK YOU ON BEHALF OF ALL THE LOCAL BUDDHISTS.

ABBESS, PLEASE DON'T EVEN MENTION IT.

THE PEOPLE OF ILAN ARE VERY SWEET AND SIMPLE.

I HAVE DECIDED TO STAY HERE!

At that time, spreading Buddhism in Taiwan was very difficult, so few people were actually true Buddhists.

Due to the civil unrest and fear generated by the February 28 incident, the appearance and activities of a young monk from Mainland China drew the attention and suspicion of the local Taiwanese.

So Hsing Yun, like many others, was being constantly watched.

TAT

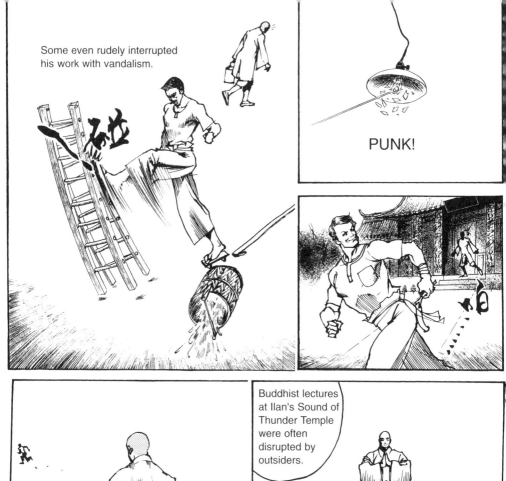

Some even rudely interrupted his work with vandalism.

PUNK!

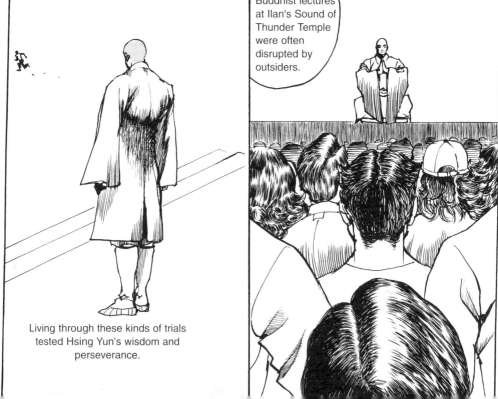

Buddhist lectures at Ilan's Sound of Thunder Temple were often disrupted by outsiders.

Living through these kinds of trials tested Hsing Yun's wisdom and perseverance.

HONK!

CLANG!

Making loud noises, they tried disrupting as much as possible.

HA HA HA...

Hsing Yun immediately sensed what he must do and rising quickly...

...turned out the light.

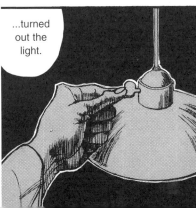

79

Although in Ilan only a short time...

...Hsing Yun came to understand the customs and character of the people.

He realized that if these people could accept Buddhism, they would become excellent future disciples.

I'M DETERMINED TO TEACH HUMANISTIC BUDDHISM HERE, STEP BY STEP.

Although young and all alone, Hsing Yun managed to do the work of five people. He was constantly busy, both outside and inside the temple.

He hosted the 7-day Amitabha Ceremony and decorated the Buddha Hall himself...

...as well as cooked special mixed vegetable soup.

VAROOM!

SWOOSH!

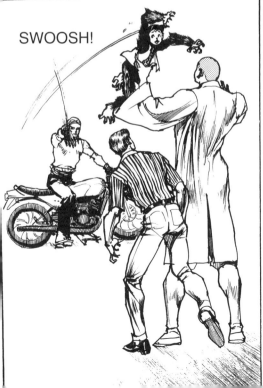

HUH!

MY NAME IS JUSTICE, AND PEOPLE ALSO CALL ME "VEGGIE MAN" IN THE MARKET.

IN THE FUTURE, IF ANYONE GIVES YOU A HARD TIME, JUST LET ME KNOW.

Soon all of Ilan was touched by the dedicated hard work of the young Hsing Yun.

SOUND OF THUNDER TEMPLE
"You are welcome to join us for a Buddhist lecture."

In order to spread Buddhism among the local people, Hsing Yun established Buddhist chanting sessions.

Next on his agenda was attracting and educating young people...Hsing Yun himself did not have a very good ear for music.

But he knew that the young liked music and singing...

...and gathering in order to make friends.

Hsing Yun soon established the very first Buddhist choir in Taiwan.

He was actually planting the seeds for the next Buddhist generation.

Special tutoring groups were formed for junior and senior high school students.

The students were quite poo[r] and unable to pa[y] the usual tutoria[l] fees. Hsing Yu[n] invited a teache[r] to instruct them free of charge.

Hard work produces
wonderful results.

In 1958, Tibetan Buddhists under the Dalai Lama were rising against communist oppression.

On April 8, a lantern parade was held to celebrate the growth of Buddhism and the Buddha's birthday.

Every district in Ilan was represented by a float.

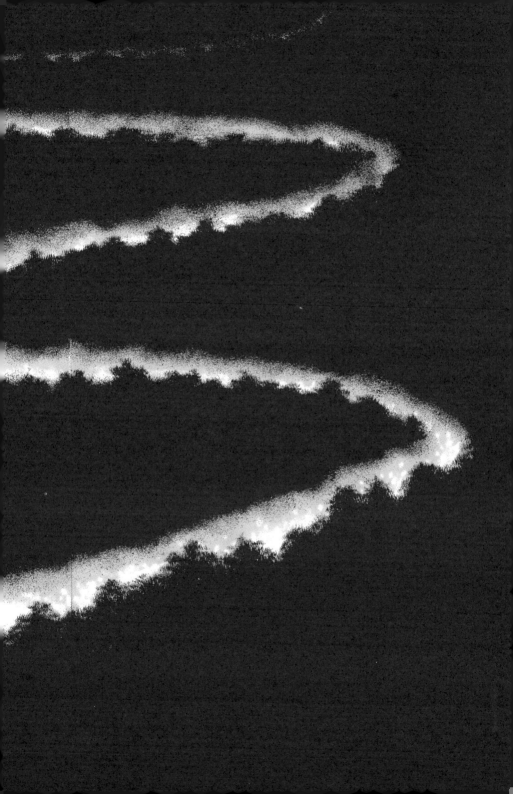

Homes were left empty as everyone in the city turned out to watch the parade.

The residents were delighted with their first-ever Buddhist parade.

And it was the first time many Buddhists had ever experienced a sense of teamwork and belonging.

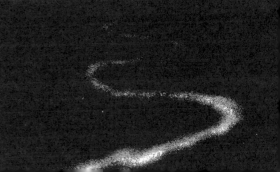

Throughout the next twelve years, the monk from the "outside" came to feel completely at home in the city and hills of Ilan.

WHEN I ARRIVE, NO ONE HAS TO MEET ME, WHEN I LEAVE, NO ONE NEEDS TO SAY GOODBYE...

...THAT, TO ME, IS THE TRUE FEELING OF HOME!

Later travel would take him far and wide, but his heart was always in Ilan.

Most of Hsing Yun's excellent disciples came from Ilan.

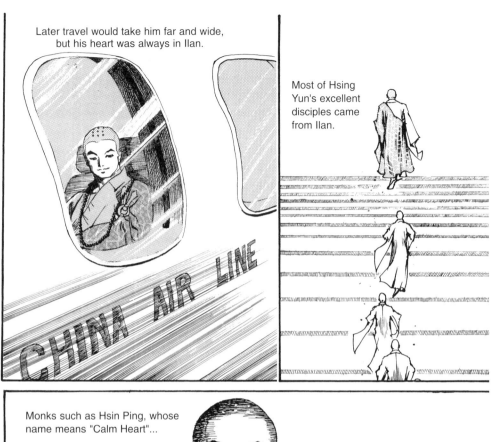

Monks such as Hsin Ping, whose name means "Calm Heart"...

...and nuns such as Tzu Chuang, "Magnificent Compassion"; Tzu Hui, "Kind Compassion"; Tzu Chia, "Excellent Compassion"; and Tzu Jung, "Tolerant Compassion."

These disciples became important leaders and decision makers in the Fo Guang Shan community.

Without the Sound of Thunder Temple...

Fo Guang Shan, which means "Buddha's Light Mountain," would not exist.

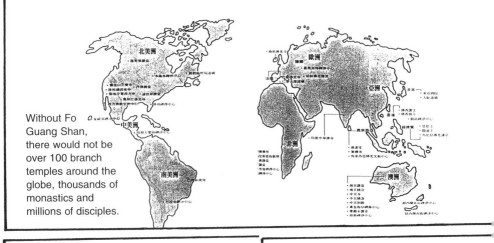

Without Fo Guang Shan, there would not be over 100 branch temples around the globe, thousands of monastics and millions of disciples.

The city of Ilan nourished the seed of one of the century's supreme Buddhist masters...

...and contributed to the flourishing of the Fo Guang Shan endeavor.

The modernization of Buddhism in Taiwan had its roots in beautiful Ilan!

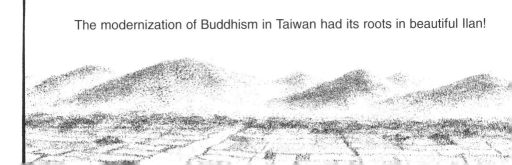

Part IV
**A NEW ERA
FOR BUDDHISM**

Charming and lovely as Ilan was, Hsing Yun
realized he needed more space and more
resources in order to spread Buddhism.

His attention eventually turned towards
an unlikely hilly plot in Kaohsiung.

In 1964,
Hsing Yun
established a
Buddhist college
on Long Life
Mountain.

Soon the place was
filled with students
eager to study, so
many, that the
classroom was
overflowing.

His plan was to build a modern
monastery to spread the Dharma,
incorporating educational and
cultural functions, based on his
experience of monasteries in
Mainland China.

When others heard of his heartfelt wish, they quickly joined in support.

Wisely, Hsing Yun chose Bamboo Grove in Big Tree Village in Kaohsiung to be the new home of Fo Guang Shan.

MASTER, FORGET THIS PLACE! WHO WOULD EVER WANT TO COME HERE TO PAY RESPECTS TO THE BUDDHA!

YOU BET! MASTER HIMSELF WILL BE THE ONLY ONE WHO WILL BOTHER TO COME HERE!

I AGREE! NO ONE IN THEIR RIGHT MIND WOULD COME HERE.

Facing the criticism with those who had come with him, Hsing Yun realized they weren't about to change their minds.

However, in Hsing Yun's mind, he knew a lot about opportunity, and he refused to back down.

Construction on the over-grown site proved incredibly difficult...

...They were like pioneers, carving out a clearing within the dense bamboo forest.

Drawing with a stick in the dirt, Hsing Yun showed the builders the plan he had in mind. Gesturing and drawing together, they drew up their plans for leveling the hilly location.

At that time no roads had been built, so a bulldozer could not be used.

AAARGGGH!

The students of the Buddhist college helped to dig and clear the site.

AAARGGGH!

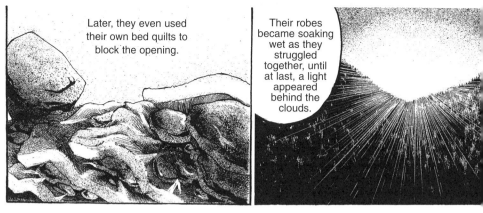

Later, they even used their own bed quilts to block the opening.

Their robes became soaking wet as they struggled together, until at last, a light appeared behind the clouds.

Hsing Yun stood on the balcony.

Not only does Fo Guang Shan have a wonderful master plan...

...but the architecture itself is breathtaking...

...the buildings are beautifully decorated.

THE MAIN BUDDHA HALL
IS GRAND AND SPACIOUS.

The Buddha statues on the grounds are magnificent, calling to mind the Chan saying,

*In one flower,
the world is seen.
In one leaf,
the Tathagata.*

In Hsing Yun's hands, Fo Guang Shan has developed into a world famous Buddhist site. Greatness has appeared from what appeared to be nothing.

In these past thirty years, many have come to the mountain to pay respects to the Buddha, both men and women, as individuals or in groups.

WOW!
IT IS SO
WONDERFUL!

Countless famous people from around the world have come to visit as well.

In 1978, Hsing Yun became the president of the International Buddhist Progress Society, and received an honorary Ph.D. from the American University of Oriental Studies.

In order to spread the teachings of Buddhism in the West, Hsing Yun established Hsi Lai Temple; the temple's name in English means "Coming West Temple."

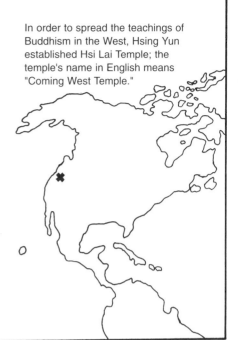

Hsing Yun established Hsi Lai Temple as an international multicultural center. For American Buddhists, Hsi Lai Temple is a peaceful place for both body and mind.

The monastic disciples of Hsing Yun come from over thirty different countries. This is proof that Buddhism has truly become international.

The small step taken to develop Hsi Lai Temple is actually a great step in the development of Buddhism.

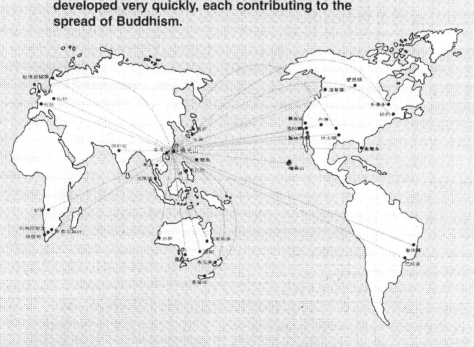

Many of the overseas temples look to Hsi Lai as an example. The branch temples around the world developed very quickly, each contributing to the spread of Buddhism.

Smiling throughout, Hsing Yun waved to the disciples, heartfully thanking all of them.

Although so many wanted him to stay, Hsing Yun knew it was time for him to go.

He wanted to follow the Fo Guang Shan rule about leaving at the right time, as well as step down from his tremendous administrative duties.

This would leave him free to pursue his own practice, educate his disciples, and continue his writing.

Fo Guang Shan has accomplished many things in the ten years since Hsing Yun stepped down. Hsing Yun has also created for himself a wonderful second career.

Hsing Yun's Chan Talks are a popular feature on the Taiwan Television Channel.

The Fo Guang Buddhist Dictionary has won the Golden Cauldron Award for outstanding publications.

The Fo Guang Shan Cultural and Educational Foundation was established, and the Buddha's Light International Association won the award for outstanding service organization in Taiwan.

Another popular television channel carries **Hsing Yun's Dharma Words**.

Two years in a row, Fo Guang Shan has won the Outstanding Social and Educational Award of R.O.C.

President Li Teng-hui asked Fo Guang Shan to assist in relief efforts during the disaster of August 12th.

Hsing Yun's Diary, as well as many other works by Hsing Yun have been published.

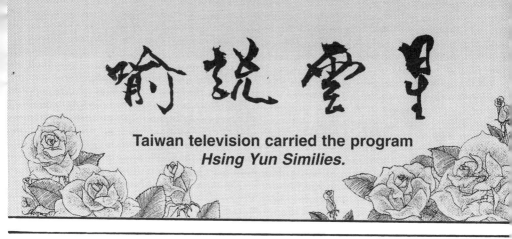

喻說雲星

Taiwan television carried the program
Hsing Yun Similies.

Hsing Yun has became the Honorary
President of the World Fellowship of
Buddhists. He is also the president of
the BLIA World Headquarters.

SWOOSH!

Strong and robust even in his senior years, Hsing Yun continues to spread Buddhism around the world, wishing that all might have the chance to encounter these teachings.

Constantly working to share Humanistic Buddhism wherever he goes...

IF BUDDHISM IS NOT CONNECTED TO OUR DAILY LIFE, WHAT USE IS IT?

100 years ago, the British used warfare to establish their empire around the world.

They were aware that the "sun never sets on the British Empire."

100 years later, a great Chinese monk, with the compassion, wisdom, vow, and practice of the bodhisattva...

...aided by the Buddha's Light International Association, has sown the seeds of Buddhism with peace and equanimity, spreading the Dharma throughout the world, and establishing universal Buddhism.

Now, wherever the sun rises, there is Dharma.

Indeed, the greatest contribution of Venerable Master Hsing Yun is that Chinese Buddhism has been carried successfully not only to Taiwan, but to the world.

In the midst of the desert, the flowers and fruit of the pure land now bloom, spreading modern Buddhism.

How does this famous Buddhist master view his entire life? This is how he describes himself.

*I embrace the vow to
deliver all beings;
I float like an untied
boat in the Dharma sea.
If you ask what lifetime
merits I have,
They are the Buddha's
light across the land.*

SWOOSH!

While learning to use the dictionary in the monastery, Hsing Yun stumbled upon the term "star nebula," defined as huge, ancient, without bound. Contemplating the union of countless cloud-like stars before the universe took form, Hsing Yun was inspired to adopt the words as his own. Vowing to bring light to those in the dark, he ventured to be always above and beyond care and bondage.

THIS IS STAR AND CLOUD!

Chronology of Venerable Master Hsing Yun

1927   Born on the 22nd day of the 7th month of the lunar calendar in Jiangdu, Jiangsu province, [China]. Named Li Kuoshen. Father Li Huicheng, mother Liu Yuying. Third of four children, with an older brother and sister, and a younger brother.

1931   Became vegetarian alongside maternal grandmother, a Buddhist.

1934   Entered rural school.

1937   His father went on a business trip to Nanjing and turned up missing.

1938   Went midway to Nanjing with mother in quest of his father, took the tonsure under Venerable Master Zhikai at Qixia Temple. Given the Dharma names Wuche and Jinjue. Became a disciple of the 48th generation of the Linji division in Chan Buddhism.

1941   Ordained at Qixia Temple.

1944   Studied at Tianning Temple, Changzhou.

1945   Transferred to Jiaoshan Buddhist College.

1947   Arrived in Dajue Temple, Baita Mountain. Became principal of White Pagoda Elementary School. Founded monthly *Raging Billows* with schoolmate Master Zhiyong. Was arrested by the communists.

1948   Became director of Huazhang Temple, Nanjing. Edited "Splendid Light," supplement of newspaper *Xubao*.

1949   Arrived in Chilung, Taiwan, with monastic relief group. Arrested with Master Cihang and others on allegations of subversive activities and incarcerated for twenty-three days.

1950   Took shelter at Yuankuang Temple, Chungli, under Master Miaokuo. Also stood guard in the mountains around Fayun Temple Miaoli, where he authored *Singing in Silence*, his first work.

1951   Took charge of academic affairs in a Buddhist seminar conducted by Venerable Daxing. Edited *Life Monthly* and learned Japanese.

1952   Elected an executive of the Chinese Buddhist

Association. Raised funds for emergency relief for the flood in Hualien.

1953 Spoke on the Dharma at Leiyin Temple, Ilan, at the invitation of Li Chueh-ho. Published *Discourse on Avalokitesvara's Universal Gate Chapter*.

1954 Stationed at Leiyin Temple and started teaching in rural areas and prisons. Venerables Tzu Chuang, Tzu Hui, and Tzu Jung took refuge in the Triple Gems.

1955 Taught around Taiwan while promoting the reprinting of the Buddhist Canon. Suffered severe arthritis in the legs. Published *Biography of Sakyamuni Buddha*, the first-ever hardback Buddhist text published in Taiwan.

1956 Completed the lecture hall for the Ilan Chanting group. Founded the first kindergarten, Ciai, and tutored in arts and sciences, Kuang-hua. Taught in prisons.

1957 Published *National Master Yulin*. Founded and became chief-editor of *Awakening the World*, a magazine which was published three times a month.

1958 Conducted the Dharma function for the preservation of the nation held by the Chinese Buddhist Association in Taipei. Venerable Hsin Ping was tonsured.

1959 Supported the Tibetan Buddhist movement against communist suppression. Organized the first float parade in celebration of the Buddha's birthday. Established the Buddhist Cultural Service in Sanchung, Taipei. Published *Biography of Sakyamuni Buddha's Ten Great Disciples*.

1960 Published *The Enlightenment Sutra*.

1961 Became publisher of *Buddhism Today*. Led the Ilan youth choir and cut the first six Buddhist records in Taiwan.

1962 Took over the publishing of *Awakening the World*.

1963 Organized a Buddhist visiting group with Venerable Pai Sheng and toured India, Thailand, Malaysia, Singapore, the Philippines, Japan, and Hong Kong. Met with King Bhumibol Adulyadej of Thailand, President Diosdado

Macapagal of the Philippines, etc. Petitioned for the release of 700 Chinese and rescued two fishing vessels in Kaohsiung.

1964　Completion of Shoushan Temple, Kaohsiung, followed by the founding of Shoushan Buddhist College. Established a school of commerce named Chih-kuang with Venerables Wu I and Nan T'ing. Published a book of travels and a range of bilingual Buddhist texts in Chinese and English.

1965　Published a series of lectures titled *Awakening the World*.

1967　Construction began on Fo Guang Shan. Shoushan Buddhist College renamed Tungfang Buddhist College. Took over a Christian mission building, which was turned into a home for the aged and poor.

1969　Held the first Buddhist summer camp for college-level students. Founded the first Buddhist Sunday School for children. Built Pilgrim's Lodge at Fo Guang Shan.

1970　Founded Tatz'u Nursery. Established pilgrims' group.

1971　Completion of the Great Compassion Shrine, followed by the blessing of the Buddha's image. Founded P'u-men Vihara, Taipei, which later became P'u-men Temple. Elected president of Sino-Japanese Buddhist Association.

1972　Introduced the constitution of Fo Guang Shan's Committee of Religious Affairs.

1973　Chiang Ching-Kuo, head of the executive council, visited Fo Guang Shan for the first time. Basketball court at Tung Shan officially opened. Founded Fo Guang Shan Ts'ung-lin College, which was renamed Chinese Buddhist Research Institute.

1974　Groundbreaking for Fu-shan Temple, Changhua.

1975　Foundation laid for the Great Welcoming Buddha and the Main Shrine. Conducted a three-day lecture at the National Arts Hall, which was the first-ever Buddhist lecture held in the halls of government.

1976　Attended the U.S. bicentennial festivities and taught the Dharma. Ran Buddhist summer camp for seniors and started an English Buddhist center. Was founding publisher of *Fo Guang Scholarly Journal*. Launched a clinic at Shoushan Temple, Kaohsiung, and Pu-men Hospital.

1977   Lectured at Chung-shan Hall, Taipei. Founded Pu-men High School. Established the editing and publishing center for the Fo Guang Buddhist Canon. Chinese Buddhist Research Institute and University of Oriental Studies, U.S.A. became sister schools. Ten Thousand Buddhas Triple Platform Ordination deemed a preceptoral model.

1978   After becoming president of R.O.C., Chiang Ching-Kuo visited Fo Guang Shan again. Held Dharma function for the preservation of the nation in Dr. Sun Yat-sen Memorial Hall. Raised funds for the establishment of a Chinese Buddhist Youth Association. Received honorary Ph.D. from University of Oriental Studies. Became first president of International Buddhist Progress Society. Raised funds for the establishment of Hsi Lai Temple.

1979   In view of strained diplomatic ties between Taiwan and the United States, held Buddhist concert at Dr. Sun Yat-sen Memorial Hall to raise funds for a national foundation of self-sufficiency. Launched *Universal Gate* magazine; first Buddhist program, *Sweet Dew* televised. Led pilgrimage to India. Held first Buddhist summer camp for children. *National Master Yulin* adapted for the stage at the National Arts Hall.

1980   Produced the first set of Buddhist bookmarks and calendar. Became director of Chinese Culture University's Indian Research Institute. Telecast of the program *Gate of Faith*.

1981   Held Buddhist summer camp for mothers. Taught Buddhist philosophy at Donghai University.

1982   Fo Guang Shan became brother temples with Tongdo Sa, Korea. Conducted the 5th International Buddhist Scholars' Conference.

1983   Honored by the ministries of legal affairs and education for outstanding educational achievements.

1984   Met the Dalai Lama. Established a mobile clinic to offer free medical care. Founded the first Buddhist city college at P'u-hsien

Temple, Kaohsiung.

1985 Held World Buddhist Youth Scholars' Conference. Passed the abbotship of Fo Guang Shan to Venerable Hsin Ping. Practiced in isolation at Hsi Lai Temple, Los Angeles. Served as executive officer of the Chinese-Tibetan Cultural Association of the Republic of China. *The Platform Sutra of the Sixth Patriarch* televised, as well as *Venerable Master Hsing Yun's Lecture Series*, which was honored by the Department of Information.

1986 World Sutric and Tantric Buddhist Conference held at Fo Guang Shan. Took office as advisor of nationalist party affairs. Launched new annual lecture series at Kaohsiung Chungcheng Cultural Center.

1987 Became founding president of the American Buddhist Youth Association. Visited Chinese Buddhist Temple, Sarnath, India. *Hsing Yun's Chan Talk* televised.

1988 Inauguration of Hsi Lai Temple, where the 16th World Fellowship of Buddhists Conference and the 7th World Fellowship of Buddhist Youth Conference were held. Conducted purifying service for the opening of California State and city of Los Angeles meetings. Taught in Hong Kong for the first time at the City Hall. Held the first alms-round fundraising event for the Fo Guang Shan Cultural and Educational Foundation. Traveled to northern Thailand with medical team and taught there. The *Fo Guang Encyclopedia* honored by the Department of Information.

1989 Held International Chan Conference at Fo Guang Shan. On his first homecoming in four decades, paid homage to ancestral stupas in Ch'i-hsia and visited his mother in Chiangtu. The Dalai Lama was a guest at Hsi Lai Temple. *Hsing Yun's Ch'an Talk* honored by the department of information. Spoke on the Dharma to the armed forces and their respective academies.

1990 Invited to attend the inauguration of U.S. President George Bush. Received his mother at Fo Guang Shan and Xu Jiatun, head of the New China News Agency in Hong Kong, at Hsi Lai Temple. Began an annual three-day lecture at Hung-hom Coliseum, Hong Kong. Went on lecture tour in England, Holland, Belgium, France, Switzerland, Austria, Yugoslavia, and Italy. Plans for the construction of International Buddhist Association of Australia under way on a thirty-six acre property donated by the city of Sydney, Australia.

1991 Hsi Lai University, temporarily housed at Hsi Lai Temple, opened. Founded Buddha's Light International Association, R.O.C. and raised funds for floods on the mainland. Hospitalized for a broken right thigh. *Hsing Yun Dharma Words* televised. Established a branch temple in a chateau outside Paris and began the spread of the Dharma in Europe.

1992 Buddha's Light International Association established and its first meeting held at Hsi Lai Temple. Devotee Chang ShengKai donated his own residence for the establishment of the first branch temple in South America, I.B.P.S. Do Brasil. Was requested to put up a temple in Johannesburg, South Africa by Dr. Hennie Senekal--the first step in the spread of the Dharma in Africa. Honored for a second year by the ministry of education for outstanding educational undertakings. Fo Guang Shan Cultural and Educational Foundation also honored.

1993 *National Master Yulin* televised on CTS. Second B.L.I.A. World Conference held in Taipei. Registration of Fo Guang University officially approved by the Ministry of Education, followed by groundbreaking ceremony in Linmei, Chiao-hsi, in Ilan county. Buddha's Light International Association named the most outstanding social organization in Taiwan.

1994 Extensive fundraising for Fo Guang University through art auctions. Taipei Temple inaugurated. Received key to the city and honorary citizenship from Austin, Texas. Third B.L.I.A. World Conference held in Vancouver, Canada. Fo Guang Shan provided emergency relief for the massive floods in August at the request of President Li Teng-hui. *Hsing Yun Says* opened on TTV. *Diary of Hsing Yun* published in twenty volumes. Ten  monastics of African descent tonsured. Held honorary presidency of World Fellowship of Buddhists and presidency of B.L.I.A.

1995 *Handing Down the Light: The Biography of Venerable Master Hsing Yun*, authored by Fu Chiying, was published by Commonwealth Publishing. Received a special award, the Buddhist equivalent to the Noble Prize, from the "National Indian Buddhist Ceremony." Venerable Hsin Ping passed away. Presented copies of *The Buddhist Volumes* to devotees, Dharma lecturers, and benefactors of Fo Guang Shan.

1996 Invited to preside over the Candlelight and Triple Gem Refuge Ceremony, held at Shah Alam Stadium, Kuala Lumpur, attended by at least 80,000 people. Played host to U.S. Vice-President Al Gore's visit to Hsi Lai Temple. Taiwan's President, Li Teng-hui presented congratulatory gift to commemorate Fo Guang Shan's 30th Anniversary. Mother, Madam Li, passed away at Hsi Lai Temple at ninety-five years of age. Founded Nan Hua Management College.

1997 Had the "Religious Dialogue of the Century" with Pope John Paul II in Vatican City, Italy. Presided over the official installation ceremony of Venerable Hsin Ting as the 3ʳᵈ Abbot of Fo Guang Shan. Honored by both the R.O.C's internal affairs, and foreign relation ministries with special recognition awards. Offical release of *You Qing You Yi*. Selected as one of the ten most influential people by the Canadian 1470AM Chinese radio station's Sunshine Project. *National Master Yulin* and *Handing Down the Light* selected as ten best publications. Received the *"Hua Shia"* first class scroll.

1998 Retired as BLIA R.O.C president. Wu Pohsiung formally appointed as new president of BLIA R.O.C. Presided over the first combined Theravada, Mahayana, and Tibetan Triple Platform Ordination Ceremony in Bodhgaya, India. Visited Thailand to officially receive  the Buddha's Tooth Relic. Officiated at Hsi Lai University's 1ˢᵗ commencement ceremony. First official meeting with Malaysian Prime Minister, Dr. Mahathir Mohammad in Kuala Lumpur, Malaysia. Ground breaking ceremony in Houston, Texas. Mayor of Houston declared June 20 as Venerable Master Hsing Yun Day. On his 72ⁿᵈ birthday, presented with a special birthday gift by Taiwan's vice-president, Lian Zhan.

1999 President Li Tenghui visited Fo Guang Shan to officially mark the start of the Fo Guang Shan Buddhist Music Concert tour in Taiwan. During the visit, President Li also announced that the Buddha's Birthday on April 8 will be a National Holiday in Taiwan. Led the Buddhist Music Concert tour in Europe for a month. Conducted prayer and memorial services for victims of the Taiwan 921 earthquake, which occurred during the European tour. Initiated the establishment of Emergency Relief centers around the world. Published *Hsing Yun's Hundred Saying Series*, and *The Buddhism Textbook*.

What is Humanistic Buddhism?

Humanistic Buddhism is not a new teaching nor a new doctrine. Over 2,600 years ago, Sakyamuni Buddha, the founder of Buddhism, became enlightened in his 31st year on earth. Following the river Ganges, he traveled all over India, visiting all the kingdoms along the way and teaching on a daily basis. Tirelessly, he taught everyone, regardless of their caste. Kings, courtiers, merchants, servants, scholars, commoners, and even criminals were all equal in his eyes.

Buddha was born into this world, he sought the true nature of life during his time in this world, he attained enlightenment while in this world, he taught people in this world, and he entered nirvana while in this world. Sakyamuni Buddha is a Buddha for all of us in this world. His teachings truly embody Humanistic Buddhism.

The Humanistic Buddhism promoted by Fo Guang Shan comes from the direct teaching lineage of the Buddha. It emphasizes family harmony, personal peace, and societal prosperity. When we are able to incorporate the Dharma into our daily lives, contentment will naturally follow. This, in turn, will be gradually followed by a deeper realization of our true nature.

Over thirty years ago, many opposed Master Hsing Yun's plan to teach Humanistic Buddhism. Now, many Taiwanese Buddhist sects are promoting Humanistic Buddhism as their own. From Asia to Europe to America to Australia to Africa, wherever there are Buddhists, one will inevitably encounter Humanistic Buddhism. Humanistic Buddhism has become synonymous with modern, enlightened, progressive, and practical Buddhism.

Fo Guang Shan introduced Humanistic Buddhism to the community and provided a model for how the teachings can be integrated into all aspects of life. Politics, economics, education, cultural events, relationships, the environment, and in fact, all of life's activities can benefit from an engaged Buddhist practice. Now that Buddhism has transformed its role and function in society, it is ready to move forward to meet the challenges of international and global demands.

Thirty-Three Years of Fo Guang Shan (Buddha's Light Mountain)

Beginning the sowing of Bodhi seeds –
Founding Master Arrives in Taiwan

In 1949, after the Communists took over Mainland China, Master Hsing Yun arrived in Taiwan. Unfamiliar with the local dialect and completely alone, he began the difficult task of spreading the Dharma. At that time, Taiwan had recently been returned to the Chinese after a lengthy Japanese occupation. The local economy was poor, martial law was strict, and people were constantly fearful; living was not easy. Buddhism was mired in superstition and monks were busy tending to the dead and not to the living. Most people regarded all temples to be the same, making no differentiations between Taoism and Buddhism. It was a difficult and turbulent time for a teacher of Buddhism, but Master Hsing Yun was not discouraged; he set out to clear the Buddhist path and promote Humanistic Buddhism.

In 1952, upon the invitation of devotees, Master Hsing Yun moved to a simple and rustic mountain village called Ilan to spread bodhi seeds. The people of Ilan were honest and sincere about embracing Buddhism and responded to Master Hsing Yun's kindness and efforts by forming committees, choirs, kindergartens, and Sunday schools. The helpful and diligent people of Ilan were pioneers in the establishment of Humanistic Buddhism in Taiwan.

Setting the foundation and building a spiritual home
The First Decade

In 1964, Master Hsing Yun saw the need to nurture a new generation of Buddhists. To create a solid foundation for the long-term growth of Buddhism, he first founded a Buddhist college in Kaohsiung's Shoushan (Mt.

Long Life), to educate young people who were interested in Buddhism. The number of students grew so rapidly that within a few years, the number of admissions outpaced the college's capacity.

Consequently, in 1967, with the intention of improving the study environment, Master Hsing Yun purchased a thirty-acre piece of mountainous land in remote Mazhu Yuan. The purchase was made with strong opposition by the Master's followers. To ease their doubts and set an example, Master Hsing Yun led his disciples in preparing the land for the construction of Fo Guang Shan. He filled ditches, mixed concrete, removed rocks, and built walls; working through all kinds of weather and never complaining of hardship or exhaustion. After a few years, they witnessed the culmination of their incredible efforts in the completion of Fo Guang Shan. In amazement, they beheld its magnificent buildings and elegant gardens. Fo Guang Shan became a new spiritual base and headquarters for Buddhism, locally, nationally, and internationally.

Proclaiming the Faith and Establishing the School –
The Second Decade

The mission of Fo Guang Shan is to proclaim Buddhism. Master Hsing Yun set forth the following four principles: "Educate the young, improve culture, benefit society, and purify the mind." He also created the following Fo Guang motto: "Give others confidence, give others joy, give others convenience, and give others hope." He also established the guidelines for practice and the rules of behavior. In addition, he organized the activities and ignited the momentum for moving Buddhism into a new era.

Among the activities and opportunities for practice at Fo Guang Shan are short-term monastic retreats, lay study groups, eight precept retreats, inner-city academies, triple platform full ordination, daily almsround, sutra sessions, printing of shastras, publication of books and magazines, pilgrimages, chanting groups, and international scholastic discussions. Fo Guang Shan became the leader in popularizing the practice of Buddhism in daily life and in reaching out to all the cities and villages of Taiwan.

Passing the Torch and Assisting the Populace –
The Third Decade

After twenty years of hard work, Master Hsing Yun felt that he had achieved the goal of modernizing Buddhism from an old tradition to a spiritual path in tune with contemporary trends. His keen insight, innovative ideas, and tireless efforts helped to shift the focus from self-centered to socially conscious, from meditative to productive, from provincial to global, from passive to active, from hermetic to altruistic, from renunciation to involvement, from monastery to family, from deliberation to action, and from charity to faith. Master Hsing Yun also brought the Buddhist teachings to both young and old alike, making it accessible to all generations. The foundation of Taiwanese Buddhism is now firmly established. In 1987, Master Hsing Yun announced his retirement, and in the tradition of great masters of the past, he passed the torch to his first disciple, Venerable Hsin Ping, as the succeeding abbot of Fo Guang Shan.

After his retirement as the abbot of Fo Guang Shan, Master Hsing Yun devoted his life to developing Buddhism globally. He spoke in many countries, in North America, Europe, Asia, and in Australia. Over the years, Master Hsing Yun patiently taught everyone, listened to their sorrows, and helped them find peace. He also created the Buddha's Light International Association (BLIA), Hsi Lai University, Fo Guang University, and the International Buddhist Progress Society. People everywhere gained a chance to learn Buddhism and Fo Guang Shan became a pilgrimage destination for many Buddhists around the world.

Continuing the Tradition and Being a Role Model for the Future –
The Future Ahead

In thirty-three years, Fo Guang Shan not only changed the look and texture of Buddhism but also set a new course for both Chinese Buddhism and Bud-dhism globally. It has faithfully served the community and the society. To continue the work of Buddhism and attract more followers to the teachings, the administrative board of Fo Guang Shan decided that after thirty years of service, Fo Guang Shan should be closed to the public.

Closing Fo Guang Shan to the public does not mean that the door to Buddhism is also closed. On the contrary, with the closure, its work can move toward a newer, deeper, and broader phase. Fo Guang Shan is continuing to work quietly and diligently in promoting education, meditation, cultural activities, and other pursuits for the benefit of society. It is focusing on broadening Buddhism to meet contemporary challenges so it can truly become a refuge for all the people in the world and a guiding light for all who are lost. This is the vision and the ultimate goal that Master Hsing Yun's life is devoted to, befitting his motto, "Let the Buddha's light shine through the three thousand worlds and let the Dharma flow through the five continents."

Fo Guang Shan Distribution of
Branch Temples in Taiwan, 1999

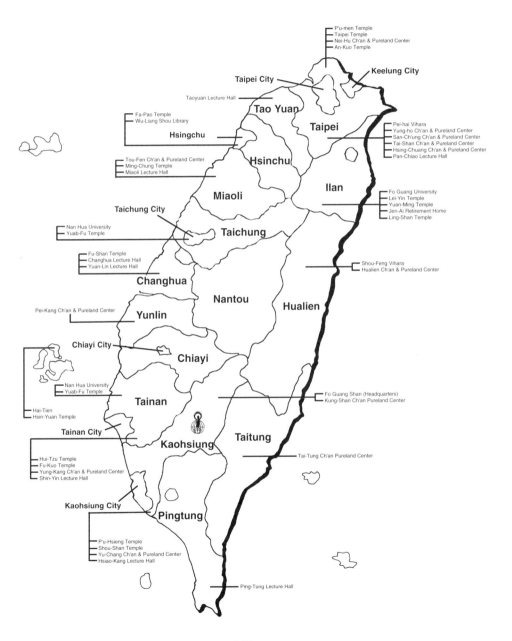

P'u-men Temple
Taipei Temple
Nei-Hu Ch'an & Pureland Center
An-Kuo Temple

Keelung City

Taipei City

Taoyuan Lecture Hall

Tao Yuan

Fa-Pao Temple
Wu-Liang Shou Library

Hsingchu

Taipei

Pei-hai Vihara
Yung-ho Ch'an & Pureland Center
San-Ch'ung Ch'an & Pureland Center
Tai-Shan Ch'an & Pureland Center
Hsing-Chuang Ch'an & Pureland Center
Pan-Chiao Lecture Hall

Tou-Fen Ch'an & Pureland Center
Ming-Chung Temple
Miaoli Lecture Hall

Hsinchu

Miaoli

Ilan

Fo Guang University
Lei-Yin Temple
Yuan-Ming Temple
Jen-Ai Retirement Home
Ling-Shan Temple

Taichung City

Nan Hua University
Yuab-Fu Temple

Taichung

Fu-Shan Temple
Changhua Lecture Hall
Yuan-Lin Lecture Hall

Shou-Feng Vihara
Hualien Ch'an & Pureland Center

Changhua

Nantou

Hualien

Pei-Kang Ch'an & Pureland Center

Yunlin

Chiayi City

Chiayi

Nan Hua University
Yuab-Fu Temple

Tainan

Fo Guang Shan (Headquarters)
Kung-Shan Ch'an Pureland Center

Hai-Tien
Hsin-Yuan Temple

Tainan City

Kaohsiung

Taitung

Hui-Tzu Temple
Fu-Kuo Temple
Yung-Kang Ch'an & Pureland Center
Shin-Yin Lecture Hall

Tai-Tung Ch'an Pureland Center

Kaohsiung City

Pingtung

P'u-Hsieng Temple
Shou-Shan Temple
Yu-Chang Ch'an & Pureland Center
Hsiao-Kang Lecture Hall

Ping-Tung Lecture Hall

Fo Guang Shan Worldwide Distribution of Branch Temples, 1999

North America

★ IBPS Edmonton
★ IBPS Vancouver
IBPS Toronto★
IBPS Montreal
IBPS Ottawa
Hawaii Buddhist Cultural Society
IBPS Kansas ★
IBPS Deerpark
American Buddhist Cultural Society, San Francisco
★ IBPS Denver
IBPS Boston
IBPS New York
IBPS Dallas ★
IBPS New Jersey
IBPS Los Angeles
IBPS Austin ★
IBPS Houston ★
San Diego Buddhist Association
IBPS Florida

Central America

IBPS Costa Rica

South America

IBPS do Brasil

IBPS Paraguay

IBPS Argentina

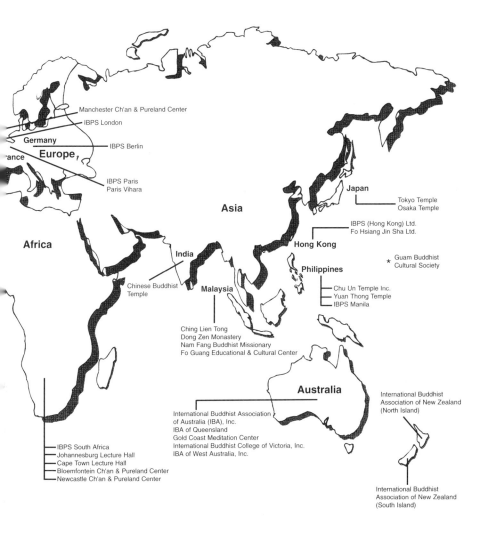

Manchester Ch'an & Pureland Center

IBPS London

Germany

IBPS Berlin

ance **Europe**

IBPS Paris
Paris Vihara

Asia

Japan

Tokyo Temple
Osaka Temple

IBPS (Hong Kong) Ltd.
Fo Hsiang Jin Sha Ltd.

Africa

India

Hong Kong

* Guam Buddhist
Cultural Society

Philippines

Chinese Buddhist
Temple

Malaysia

Chu Un Temple Inc.
Yuan Thong Temple
IBPS Manila

Ching Lien Tong
Dong Zen Monastery
Nam Fang Buddhist Missionary
Fo Guang Educational & Cultural Center

Australia

International Buddhist
Association of New Zealand
(North Island)

International Buddhist Association
of Australia (IBA), Inc.
IBA of Queensland
Gold Coast Meditation Center
International Buddhist College of Victoria, Inc.
IBA of West Australia, Inc.

IBPS South Africa
Johannesburg Lecture Hall
Cape Town Lecture Hall
Bloemfontein Ch'an & Pureland Center
Newcastle Ch'an & Pureland Center

International Buddhist
Association of New Zealand
(South Island)

145

I. Historical Buddhism in India

The ten great disciples
1 Sariputra
2 Maudgalyayana or Maudgalaputra
3 Purna
4 Subhuti
5 Katyayana
6 Mahakasyapa
7 Aniruddha
8 Upali
9 Ananda
10 Rahula

Bhiksuni
1 Mahaprajapati
2 Utapalavarna (s); Uppalavanna (p)

II. Tiantai School
1 Zhizhe
2 Zhanran
3 Zhili

III. Pure Land School
1 Lushan Huiyuan
2 Shandao
3 Daochuo
4 Yongming Yanshou
5 Lianchi
6 Shengan
7 Yinguang
8 Ouyi

IV. Mantra School
1 Milaraspa (or Milarepa)
2 Padmasambhava
3 Tsonkhapa; Tsongkhapa

V. Madhyamika School
1 Chiahsiang; Jiaxiang Jizhang
2 Sengzhao

VI. Chan School
1 Bodhidharma
2 Huike
3 Daoxin
4 Hongren
5 Huineng
6 Shenxiu
7 Huangpo Xiyun
8 Mazu Daoyi
9 Nanyue Huairang
10 Shitou Xiqian
11 Zhaozhou Congshen
12 Guishan Lingyou
13 Yangshan Huiji
14 Linji Yixuan
15 Shenhui
16 Yunmen Wenyan
17 Niutou Farong
18 Caoshan Benji
19 Dongshan Liangjie
20 Fayan Wenyi
21 Yangqi Fanghui
22 Huanglong Huinan
23 Baizhang Huaihai
24 Zibo

VII. Huayan School;
1 Fazang
2 Qiangliang Chengguan
3 Guifeng Zongmi

VIII. Mine-Only School
1 Xuanzang
2 Kuiji

3   Yuance

IX. Vinaya School
1   Daoxuan
2   Huaisu
3   Jianzhen
4   Sengyou

X. Distinguished Practice
1   Tanyao
2   Huijiao
3   Deng Yinfeng
4   Buddhasimha
5   Faxian
6   Daosheng
7   Hanshan
8   Yijing
9   Hanshan Deqing
10 Foyin Liaoyuan
11 An shigao
12 Daoan
13 Daoji

XI. Sutra Translators
1   Zhendi
2   Kumarajiva

XII. Great Contributors to Chinese Buddhism
1   Nagarjuna
2   Vasubandhu
3   Asvaghosa

XIII. Contemporary Eminent Masters
1   Xuyun
2   Manshu
3   Jichan

4   Dixian
5   Zhangjia
6   Cihang
7   Taixu
8   HsingYun
9   Hongyi
10 Jinshan

XIV. Korean and Japanse Masters
Japan
1   Ikkyu
2   Saicho
3   Shinran
4   KuKai
5   Hounen
6   Nichiren
7   Dongen
Korea
1   Chajang
2   Wonhyo
3   Uisang

專有名詞	Transliteration	Translation
黃鶴樓	Huanghe Lou	Mansion of the Golden Crane
長江	Changjiang	Yangtze River
星雲大師	Venerable Master Hsing Yun	Venerable Star and Cloud
李國深	Li Guoshen	Profound Benefit
棲霞寺	Qixia Temple	Cloud Dwelling Mountain
志開上人	Venerable Zhikai	Venerable Vast Vows
悟徹	Wuche	Thorough Enlightenment
今覺	Jinjue	Instantaneous Awakening
焦山佛學院	Zhaoshan Buddhist College	Flaming Mountain Buddhist College
圓湛法師	Venerable Yuanzhan	Venerable Profound Completeness
芝峰法師	Venerable Zhifeng	Venerable Noble Peak
智勇法師	Venerable Zhiyong	Venerable Courageous Wisdom
煮雲法師	Venerable Zhuyun	Venerable Misting Cloud
善導寺	Shandao Temple	Good Guidance Temple
圓光寺	Yuanguang Temple	Perfect Light Temple
妙果老和尚	Venerable Miaoguo	Venerable Wondrous Fruition
雷音寺	Leiyin Temple	Sound of Thunder Temple
阿義	Ayi	Justice
心平法師	Venerable Hsin Ping	Venerable Calm Heart
慈莊法師	Venerable Tzu Chuang	Venerable Magnificent Compassion
慈惠法師	Venerable Tzu Hui	Venerable Kind Compassion
慈容法師	Venerable Tzu Jung	Venerable Tolerant Compassion
慈嘉法師	Venerable Tzu Chia	Venerable Excellent Compassion
壽山寺	Shoushan Temple	Long Life Mountain Temple
大樹鄉	Ta Shu	Big Tree Village

English Publications by Venerable Master Hsing Yun

Buddha's Light Publishing:
1. Between Ignorance and Enlightenment (I)
2. Between Ignorance and Enlightenment (II)
3. Between Ignorance and Enlightenment (III)
   - A Moment, A Lifetime
4. Between Ignorance and Enlightenment (IV)
   - A Life of Pulses and Minuses
5. Between Ignorance and Enlightenment (V)
   - Let Go, Move on
6. The Awakening Life
7. Fo Guang Study
8. Sutra of the Medicine Buddha
   - with an Introduction, Comments and Prayer
9. From the Four Noble Truths to the Four Universal Vows
   - An Integration of the Mahayana and Theravada Schools
10. On Buddhist Democracy, Freedom and Equality
11. Of Benefit to Oneself and Others
    - A Critique of the Six Perfections
12. Pearls of Wisdom
    - Prayers for Engaged Living (I)
13. Pearls of Wisdom
    - Prayers for Engaged Living (II)
14. Humanistic Buddhism – a Blueprint for Life
15. Venerable Master Hsing Yun – Star and Cloud
    - Buddhist Legends of Adventure and Courage

Wisdom Publications:
16. Only a Great Rain
    - A Guide to Chinese Buddhist Meditation
17. Describing the Indescribable
    - A Commentary on the Diamond Sutra

Weatherhill, Inc.:
18. Being Good
    - Buddhist Ethics for Everyday Life
19. Lotus in a Stream
    - Basic Buddhism for Beginners

iUniverse.com, Inc.:
20. Humble Table, Wise Fare
    - Gifts for Life

Peter Lang Publishing:
21. The Lions Roar
    - Actualizing Buddhism in Daily Life and
    Building the Pure Land in Our Midst

Hsi Lai University Press:
22. Handing Down the Light
23. Perfectly Willing
24. Happily Ever After
25. How I Practice Humanistic Buddhism
26. Where is Your Buddha Nature
27. The Carefree Life
28. Humble Table, Wise Fare
    - Hospitality for the Heart (I)
29. Humble Table, Wise Fare
    - Hospitality for the Heart (I)
30. Cloud and Water

Spanish Publications by Venerable Master Hsing Yun

Portuguese Publications by Venerable Master Hsing Yun